POPULAR PRAISE

10 TIMELESS CHRISTIAN WORSHIP SONGS

EARLY ADVANCED TO ADVANCED PIANO SOLOS

ARRANGED BY CAROL TORNQUIST

ALFRED

Produced by
Alfred Music Publishing Co., Inc.
P.O. Box 10003
Van Nuys, CA 91410-0003
alfred.com

Printed in USA.

ISBN-10: 0-7390-7686-8
ISBN-13: 978-0-7390-7686-6

Cover Credits
Cross: © stock.xchng/natebernar • Sky: © stock.xchng/Mattox

(Approx. Performance Time – 2:15)

Amazing Grace
(My Chains Are Gone)

Words and Music by
Chris Tomlin and Louie Giglio

Arranged by Carol Tornquist

Moderately slow, with expression (♩ = 72)

pedal ad lib.

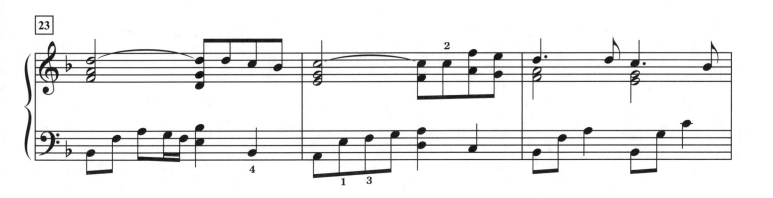

(Approx. Performance Time – 2:15)

Blessed Be Your Name

Words and Music by
Beth Redman and Matt Redman
Arranged by Carol Tornquist

Beautiful One

(Approx. Performance Time – 2:15)

Words and Music by Tim Hughes
Arranged by Carol Tornquist

pedal ad lib.

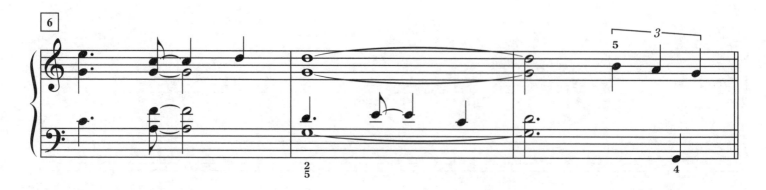

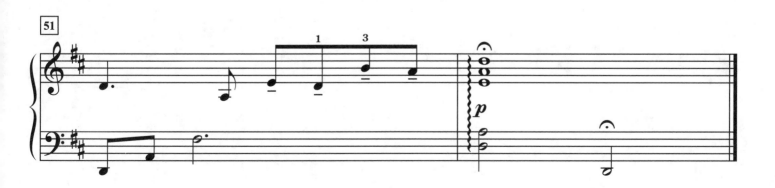

(Approx. Performance Time – 2:15)

Come, Now Is the Time to Worship

Words and Music by Brian Doerksen
Arranged by Carol Tornquist

Simply, with reverence (♩ = 54)

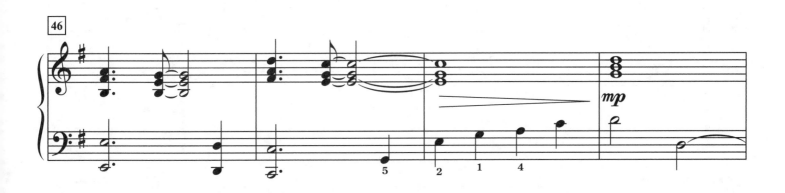

(Approx. Performance Time – 2:00)

Forever

Words and Music by Chris Tomlin

Arranged by Carol Tornquist

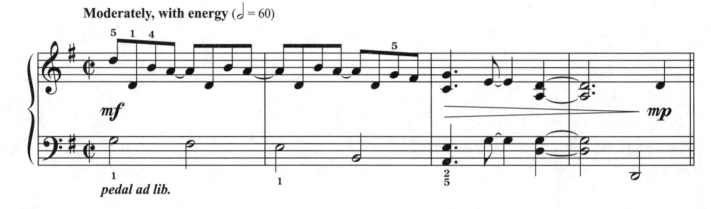

(Approx. Performance Time – 2:00)

Here I Am to Worship

Words and Music by Tim Hughes

Arranged by Carol Tornquist

(Approx. Performance Time – 2:15)

How Great Is Our God

Words and Music by
Jesse Reeves, Chris Tomlin and Ed Cash
Arranged by Carol Tornquist

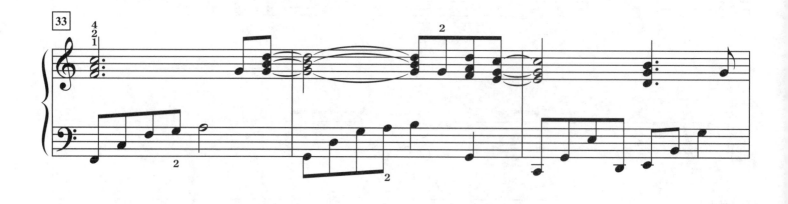

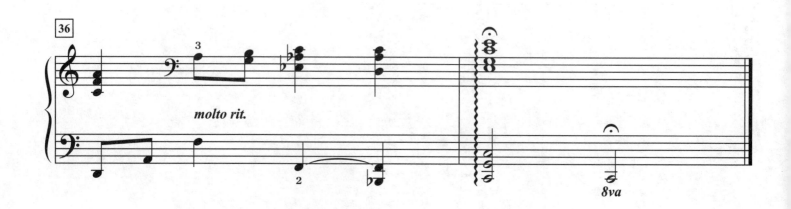

(Approx. Performance Time – 2:15)

We Fall Down

Words and Music by Chris Tomlin

Arranged by Carol Tornquist

In Christ Alone
(My Hope Is Found)

(Approx. Performance Time – 2:45)

Words and Music by
Stuart Townend and Keith Getty

Arranged by Carol Tornquist

Moderately, with confidence (♩ = 72)

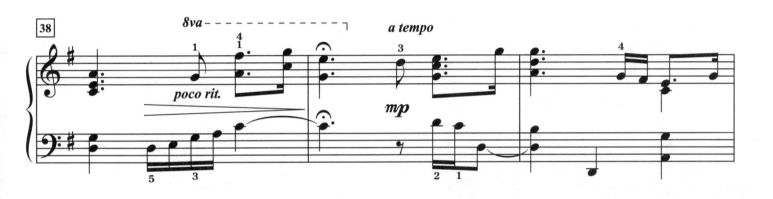

(Approx. Performance Time – 2:15)

You Are My All in All

Words and Music by Dennis L. Jernigan

Arranged by Carol Tornquist

Slowly and expressively (♩ = 66)

AMAZING GRACE (MY CHAINS ARE GONE)

Verse 1:
Amazing grace! how sweet the sound
That saved a wretch like me!
I once was lost but now am found;
Was blind, but now I see.

Chorus:
My chains are gone,
I've been set free.
My God, my Savior, has ransomed me.
And like a flood His mercy reigns,
Unending love, amazing grace.

Verse 2:
The earth shall soon dissolve like snow,
The sun forbear to shine.
But God, who called me here below,
Will be forever mine.

Chorus

BEAUTIFUL ONE

Verse 1:
Wonderful, so wonderful is Your unfailing love.
Your cross has spoken mercy over me.
No eye has seen, no ear has heard, no heart can fully know
How glorious, how beautiful You are!

Chorus:
Beautiful One I love, Beautiful One I adore.
Beautiful One, my soul must sing.

Verse 2:
Powerful, so powerful, Your glory fills the sky.
Your mighty works displayed for all to see.
The beauty of Your majesty awakes my heart to sing
How marvelous, how wonderful You are!

Chorus
Chorus

Beautiful One.
Beautiful One.

Bridge:
And You opened my eyes to wonders new;
You captured my heart with this love.
'Cause nothing on earth is as beautiful as You.
And You opened my eyes to wonders new;
You captured my heart with this love.
'Cause nothing on earth is as beautiful as You.

Chorus
Chorus

BLESSED BE YOUR NAME

Verse 1:
Blessed be Your name in the land that is plentiful,
Where Your streams of abundance flow, blessed be Your name.

Verse 2:
Blessed be Your name when I'm found in the desert place,
Tho' I walk through the wilderness, blessed be Your name.

Ev'ry blessing You pour out I'll turn back to praise.
When the darkness closes in, Lord, still I will say,

Chorus:
Blessed be the name of the Lord,
Blessed be Your name.
Blessed be the name of the Lord,
Blessed be Your glorious name!

Verse 3:
Blessed be Your name when the sun's shining down on me,
When the world's all as it should be, blessed be Your name.

Verse 4:
Blessed be Your name on the road marked with suffering,
Tho' there's pain in the offering, blessed be Your name.

Ev'ry blessing You pour out I'll turn back to praise.
When the darkness closes in, Lord, still I will say,

Chorus

Bridge:
You give and take away,
You give and take away;
My heart will choose to say,
Lord, blessed be Your name.

Chorus

COME, NOW IS THE TIME TO WORSHIP

Chorus:
Come, now is the time to worship.
Come, now is the time to give your heart.
Come, just as you are to worship.
Come, just as you are before your God.
Come.

Bridge:
One day every tongue will confess You are God.
One day every knee will bow.
Still the greatest treasure remains for those
Who gladly choose You now.

Chorus

FOREVER

Words and Music by CHRIS TOMLIN

Verse 1:
Give thanks to the Lord, our God and King.
His love endures forever.
For He is good, He is above all things.
His love endures forever.
Sing praise, sing praise!

Verse 2:
With a mighty hand and outstretched arm,
His love endures forever.
For the life that's been reborn;
His love endures forever.
Sing praise, sing praise!
Sing praise, sing praise!

Chorus:
Forever God is faithful, forever God is strong,
Forever God is with us, forever, forever!

Verse 3:
From the rising to the setting sun,
His love endures forever.
And by the grace of God we will carry on;
His love endures forever.
Sing praise, sing praise.
Sing praise, sing praise!

Chorus

HERE I AM TO WORSHIP

Words and Music by TIM HUGHES

Verse 1:
Light of the world,
You stepped down into darkness,
Opened my eyes, let me see
Beauty that made
This heart adore You,
Hope of a life spent with You.

Chorus:
Here I am to worship,
Here I am to bow down,
Here I am to say that You're my God.
You're altogether lovely,
Altogether worthy,
Altogether wonderful to me.

Verse 2:
King of all days,
Oh so highly exalted,
Glorious in heaven above,
Humbly You came
To the earth You created
All for love's sake became poor.

Chorus

Bridge:
I'll never know how much it cost
To see my sin upon that cross.
I'll never know how much it cost
To see my sin upon that cross.

Chorus

HOW GREAT IS OUR GOD

Words and Music by JESSE REEVES, CHRIS TOMLIN and ED CASH

Verse 1:
The splendor of the King
Clothed in majesty;
Let all the earth rejoice,
All the earth rejoice.
He wraps Himself in light,
And darkness tries to hide
And trembles at His voice,
And trembles at His voice.

Chorus:
How great is our God!
Sing with me
How great is our God!
And all will see how great,
How great is our God!

Verse 2:
And age to age He stands,
And time is in His hands;
Beginning and the End,
Beginning and the End.
The Godhead, three in one,
Father, Spirit, Son,
The Lion and the Lamb,
The Lion and the Lamb.

Chorus

Bridge:
Name above all names,
Worthy of all praise,
My heart will sing
How great is our God!

Chorus

IN CHRIST ALONE (MY HOPE IS FOUND)

Words and Music by STUART TOWNEND and KEITH GETTY
© 2002 THANKYOU MUSIC (PRS)
All Rights for the World excluding Europe
Administered by EMI CMG PUBLISHING
All Rights for Europe Administered by KINGSWAYSONGS.COM

In Christ alone my hope is found;
He is my light, my strength, my song;
This Cornerstone, this solid ground,
Firm through the fiercest drought and storm.
What heights of love, what depths of peace
When fears are stilled, when strivings cease;
My Comforter, my All in All;
Here in the love of Christ I stand.

In Christ alone who took on flesh;
Fullness of God in helpless babe.
This gift of love and righteousness
Scorned by the ones He came to save;
'Til on that cross as Jesus died
The wrath of God was satisfied;
For every sin on Him was laid;
Here in the death of Christ I live.

There in the ground His body lay;
Light of the world by darkness slain.
Then bursting forth in glorious day,
Up from the grave He rose again!
And as He stands in victory
Sin's curse has lost its grip on me;
For I am His and He is mine,
Bought with the precious blood of Christ!

No guilt in life, no fear in death;
This is the power of Christ in me.
From life's first cry to final breath
Jesus commands my destiny.
No power of hell, no scheme of man
Can ever pluck me from His hand;
'Til He returns or calls me home,
Here in the power of Christ I'll stand!

WE FALL DOWN

Words and Music by CHRIS TOMLIN
© 1998 WORSHIPTOGETHER.COM SONGS (ASCAP)
All Rights Administered by EMI CMG PUBLISHING

Verse:
We fall down,
We lay our crowns
At the feet of Jesus.
The greatness of mercy and love
At the feet of Jesus.

Chorus:
And we cry, "Holy, holy, holy."
And we cry, "Holy, holy, holy."
And we cry, "Holy, holy, holy is the Lamb."

YOU ARE MY ALL IN ALL

Words and Music by DENNIS L. JERNIGAN
© 1991 SHEPHERD'S HEART MUSIC, INC. (ASCAP)
All Rights Administered by PRAISECHARTS

Verse 1:
You are my strength when I am weak,
You are the treasure that I seek;
You are my all in all.
Seeking You as a precious jewel,
Lord, to give up I'd be a fool;
You are my all in all.

Chorus:
Jesus, Lamb of God, worthy is Your name!
Jesus, Lamb of God, worthy is Your name!

Verse 2:
Taking my sin, my cross, my shame,
Rising again I bless Your name;
You are my all in all.
When I fall down, You pick me up;
When I am dry, You fill my cup;
You are my all in all.

Chorus